Staccato Rhythms
of an
Iridescent Heart

Aviya Rose Publishing

Staccato Rhythms
of an
Iridescent Heart

Symphony Hale

First Edition Paperback 2023

Cover design by Roksolana Fursa

ISBN 979-8-9888113-0-5

Aviya Rose Publishing

www.symphonyhale.com

symphony_hale@outlook.com

For Juliette

I would not have found my way

Through the darkness

Without you

As my light

For you

Dear Reader

Beyond the broken

Beneath the heartache

I see you

Table of Contents

Of Heartbreak

Frantic with the ache

To claw open my flesh

And bleed this anguish

From within my soul

You were a moment of weakness

A ghostly surrender

Imprisoned within the confines of her forgotten tomorrow

Living amidst the wreckage of a yesterday illusion

A tragedy of consequence

You could neither escape nor deny

I was your means to an end

Though never your beginning

Balancing precariously

On the blade of my own desolation

You chipped away at the crumbling pieces of my resolve

Until there was no longer a lifeline from which to cling

Until the reality of my existence

Became too tangible for you to hold

I was nothing more

Than a casualty of your cowardice

And you will forever be

The executioner

Who eviscerated my hope

My words are broken

Tear stained and obsolete

Their meaning sacrificed to a shadowed revenant of time extinct

The world around me fades

Smudged with muted pastels

A dull and unfinished constellation

Hanging haphazardly amidst the midnight sky

There is a secret caveat privy only to you

A prize of which I have never been worthy

Only placated

Silenced

Smothered amongst a grayscale crowd of invalidated spirits

Mind numb

Heart in pieces

I choke on the placebos not meant to heal me

Swallow them down as they turn to ash inside my throat

I have achieved nothing in this life save for the heartache

Save for the lovely decline

Of a soul lost to madness

I lost you before I was ready

Before the ink had time to dry

Before the sands faded into the ocean

For a love so long denied

I lost you before I was ready

Before heaven came crashing down

Before your touch faded from my skin

For a love that was never found

I wait for you
I have waited for you
Through this lifetime and the last
Through countless lifetimes before
An endless existence of longing
Incomplete
Unfinished

I thought I found you once
But you floated through my fingers
Spiraled out of reach
On a breeze not meant for me to follow
A heavy emptiness fills my heart
Disquiet thoughts drifting through my mind
Holding the weight of a thousand years of possibilities
The weight of a tomorrow that may never come
I remember your heart before I knew you
Remember your voice before I heard you
But something happened
Somewhere
Within the vast hollowness of forever

And I was helpless to stop it
Now you don't see me at all
Perhaps you never truly did
But I sense you in every part of my soul
Feel your touch through every cell in my body
I see your face
Cerulean gaze
Hiding the pain of an undone mind

I cling to gossamer hope
Grasping at the unknown
Aching
For someday
Soon

A picture void of color

Fire without a flame

Fate paints a vicious picture

With a brush carved out of shame

A masterpiece awakening

From the blood of heart's demise

An easel with shattered canvas

And no way to apologize

Atoning for egregious sins

Though none of them my own

A gallery of tear stained memories

And no place that feels like home

A split second amidst infinite time

A moment never meant to last

Ethereal strands of happiness

Whispering through fingertips

Fleeting

Fragmented

Heart and soul bound

Emptied from within

Was it a mistake to love you?

As hollowed existence surrounds me

Echoing through my mind

Diaphanous dreams fade into morning

Out of reach

Forever

I don't understand how the tears continue to flow

I should be empty by now

The well

Dry and barren

But they pour from my eyes

A deluge of heartbreak

As my body vibrates with inconsolable anguish

Muscle and bone

Shattering beneath the devastating loss of your light

Heart wrenching madness rips through my soul

Shredding and tearing without regard or consequence

Every heartbeat is muffled to the world around me

Pulsing from a storm that rages within my veins

Only for me

Drowning from the inside

I balance precariously on the blade of evisceration

On a moment that could obliterate everything

Seeking Elysian silence

Unattainable

Release

Maybe I'll find you

In the next lifetime

Before your heart has been shattered

Before your soul has been closed off

Perhaps then...

Perhaps then...

You will love me

The house is too quiet

The silence

A deafening roar inside my head

I turn to you

Your sapphire gaze smoldering in the darkness

You pull me close

Lips searing a fiery trail along my neck

Whispers of longing caress my ear

Tangled limbs

Heated flesh

Nerves aflame

Every cell ignites as your touch consumes me

Breathless

I fall over the edge into oblivion

My eyes flutter open

Heart stuttering inside my chest

The stillness

Thick around me

As darkness swallows me whole

I lie here

Alone

Save for the ghost of you

Left burning within my veins

Our love was made from building blocks

And broken pieces crumbling down

Bricks with disintegrating mortar

Collapsing to the ground

Decomposing heartbeats

Impenetrable walls raised high

Esoteric moments

Of empty promises and lies

Cell by cell you broke me

Bricks chiseled from within my soul

Bleeding tears of anguish

Slipping through fingers too weak to hold

Suffocating beneath a cloud of silt

Choking on dust which coats my skin

Brick by brick you shattered us

Disappearing into the wind

Staccato rhythms of an iridescent heart

Ariose melody whispering through gossamer dreams

Souls asunder since the emergence of time

A prelude to an infinite search for crescendo

Craving a moment of completion

Yearning for a truth to hold onto

Love floats through untrained fingers

Stumbling through chords lost to aphonic song

A lullaby of heart wrenching beauty

Resonating through veins left empty and aching

Intricately woven within a haunted harmony of tears

A hollowed Symphony drowns in anguish

Waiting for her sonata finale

It started with a drop

A single tear

Cascading slowly down my cheek

Your words

Cutting across my soul

A fiery blade

Incinerating every moment

I thought to be real

A deluge of heartbreak

Spilling over the barrier of my lashes

Pouring across trembling lips

Staining what was

To midnight's waking hour

A prisoner I have become

As darkness swallows whole

And emptiness consumes

The tangent heartbeats of souls entwined

Torn apart by time's frivolous wander

Ariose tears bleeding from aphonic lips

Impalpable maunder awakens

As dawn laces the earth in aureate splendor

I close my eyes and dream of you

A case of mistaken identity

Or a malicious ruse of mimicry

You saw only what you wanted to see

I gave only what was expected of me

My heart hidden within a shadowed disguise

Self-preservation from years of betrayal and lies

Steeling my soul from your callous disregard

Love left mangled and scarred

Amidst the brambles and thorns

I wait

Shattered pieces of my heart

Scatter all around me

A name

Scorched atop my tongue

A touch

Seared into my memory

A fever

A desire

There is no cure for what ails me

Only time

An irrevocable existence

I am helpless to control

A thrumming inside my chest

A staccato rhythm within my soul

Stuttering

Faltering

As the silence of your words reverberates through me

Surging within my veins

Demons ignite from incendiary thoughts

Burning a path across tissue and bone

Open wounds

Bleeding dry

Choking on sanguinolent tears

Did you feel it?

When my breath stilled

When my heart stopped

When our love fell like ash around us

Words void of meaning

Crashing through my head

A special class of lies

Ringing with false atonement

You savor unrepentant sin

Leave me blinded by a web of deception

Shrouded beneath a blushing clover

My heart succumbs to madness

Voice choking on absolution

A silent plea

Buried beneath the wreckage

Of a broken life

Fathomless æther

Swallowing my demise

Vestige of muted light

Dappled behind gossamer shade

Eyes unfocused

Beneath the silhouette of a waking dream

A wink of effulgent desire

Burning throughout hollowed veins

I reach across the shadows

Searching for my love

Desperate for a touch

Solid and real

To free me from this loneliness

Fill the emptiness within

As the sky above breaks open

Echoing the chaos churning inside my soul

Tears rain down

Bleeding the heavens dry

Alone

I weep

Breathing in the whisper

Of your heart

Release me from this hell

In which my heart beats only for you

My soul

Emaciated

Imprisoned within this agony of suffocating desire

Breath bleeding from my lungs

Scorching through veins long empty of life

Amorphous love of tenebrous longing

You hover in the shadows

Relishing my demise

The memories are seared into my mind

Etched upon my skin

A mosaic of scars

Screaming out the story of a broken life

A kaleidoscope of time in vivid color

Running together on an endless cycle of torment and fury

Vile and bitter

The words break from my lips

I gasp

A desperate attempt to suck them back down

Lock them away in the darkest depths of my soul

But they thrash about

Scattering in the wind

Mixing and swirling with the raging storm

Lost to the deafening silence of my loneliness

They shall never reach you

You

Whose soul is blacker than my own

You

Who holds the key

To my eternal damnation

Is there a difference between delusion and dream?

A place

Caught somewhere in the midst

Where I still hold you

Where I still feel your soul

Mind awash with memories

The diagnosis from your heartbreak

Ending in ferocious consequences

A riptide dragging me under

As the murky depths fill my lungs

I succumb to the madness of longing

To the debilitating desolation

Surging through my veins

Heart screaming to a stop

A silent roar

Tearing from my chest

I surrender

When the Sidhe stopped dreaming

When the fairies fell from rest

When the nightmares taking over

Stole the breath from within my chest

A war hovers upon the horizon

Igniting anguish within my soul

As ravenous demons surround me

Flesh and bone the price I owe

A sacrificed existence

Not relinquished on a whim

As every heartbeat falters

And the world begins to dim

A voice beckons from the darkness

A love pleading for reprieve

Beneath a scarlet river of teardrops

From this hell I shall not leave

It was not heartbreak who held me prisoner

Who kept me chained

Drowning in the aftermath

Of the massacre you bestowed upon my existence

Fate

Her cruel sense of humor

Reveling in the isolation of your mind

My soul

Left in pieces

Two halves

Yearning to be whole

A twisted agony of circumstance

Forcing them apart

A vestige of silence

Piercing midnight thoughts

Deafening in their anguish

Scattered amongst the stars

It was there

Subtle

Creeping along the edge of an unhinged mind

A difference

Slight

Unnoticeable

Save for the taste

No longer the saccharin sweetness of love's desire

Laced over the tip of my tongue

Bitter

Rancid

Twisting through my insides

Bile rising

Ending in contempt

A hollow ache deep within my soul

Emptiness heavy inside my bones

Each breath strangled

At war with the scream ripping from my throat

I fight against the chains which bind me

A prisoner in my own mind

Lusting for a way out

For an end

To the chaos

Who consumes me

I have fallen into the shadow of a whispered soul

Over the edge of a mind left to madness

I have fallen beneath the surface of an endless day

Into the darkness of a night bleeding sadness

A gaunt existence

In an ethereal dream

Intricately woven

Into obscure quintessence

I want to tell you that I love you

The words sit on the tip of my tongue

Peeking between my lips

But I swallow them down

Let them hibernate in my belly

Until the ice within your soul has time to melt

Until your heart beats with life anew

Until you love me

Once again

The way you used to

A history of love

Opaque

Yet gossamer thin

Lost

Before it was found

Words with no charm

Melting

Under incandescent tears

Rivulets of ink

Smearing across pages

Translucent from time

Though never enough

A brief interlude of silence

Amidst the chaos in my head

I was never who you wanted

Severing binds choking breath

Extinguishing darkness within

Ravenously craving empty thoughts

Vanquishing immortal sin

Anguish congealing withering veins

Love vanished upon ashen skin

Faltering breath pausing time

An end with nowhere to begin

As day bleeds into desolate night

Twilight melts into impenetrable darkness

Erratic heartbeat

A staccato rhythm within my body

There is no solace for the wicked

Though I have craved it

Yearning for a moment of peace

Which does not exist

A touch

To soothe the anguish

Within my starving soul

47 is the strangest number

The number of years you have spent here

Here in this lifetime

Not waiting for me

Never waiting

I am the one held back

Suspended in this moment between awake and a dream

Alone

Isolated to my anguish

Abandoned to this purgatory of existing

Yet not

Your emotions slam through me

Thick and suffocating

I soak them in

Plagued by the delirium consuming my mind

Crawling atop my skin

Burrowing beneath my flesh

Electrifying my veins

My entire being vibrates

With the emptiness of your retreat

The hope of you

Recoiling from within my grasp

As every fiber of my existence

Rejects the notion

I am helpless to impede

Though I thought I felt you

Once

A phantom touch

Within the darkest recesses

Of my vanquished extant

But you vanished

Taking my heart with you

Too afraid to love me

Too broken to let me in

I hold my breath

Waiting for your return

Perhaps on a different day

Of violent nights

Lost to savage dreams

Dark persuasion incinerates my soul

Stains of crimson

Scorch ravaged flesh

A pretty poppy choked by thistles and thorns

Empty cavern of unshed tears

Halo of singed regret

Forgotten by all

Invisible to none

Purged by love immortal

On frayed edges of sanity

A fragile semblance of coherent cognition

My eyes dim

Vision blurs

By the abstraction of your love

Anticipated rumination

Scouring the dark recesses of forever

I hover on the brink of madness

A heart left drowning in memories

My soul extracted

Laid bare

To frivolous ruin

There is kaleidoscope of vivid heartbreak

Dancing within my chest

Whirling

Spiraling

Inebriated by the tears of malicious duality

A lustful reality of nefarious existence

I choke on the storm of molten breath

Overflowing the crevice

Hidden

Within the yellowed pages of time's forgotten promise

Buried beneath a glade of autumnal flames

My heart beats with the sultry frenzy of ominous forebode

As I crawl through this fence of razors and wire

Flesh snagging on malevolent barbs

I thrash

Immersed in the pungency of your deceit

Beseeching my spirit to prolong

Lost within a carmine haze

Of heart's forgotten song

Stranded amidst a flickering quiescence

Of unsteady time manifesting

I am magnified into an isolated existence

Unreachable outside my soul

Awkward in my own skin

Inadequate

Unworthy

Density within the air

Growing thick and haunting

Every breath

Rasping between quivering lips

Solder me or sever me

Love me or let me go

Fog rolls over the earth

In gossamer waves upon the frigid landscape

At water's edge

I wait

Your voice whispering along the breeze

A sweet caress across my skin

From the shadows a kelpie emerges

Out of the darkness

Into this hostile existence

Come to drag me from my vicious hell

Or back to it

If that's where I belong

A moment of sweet reprieve

Forever lost

I drown in the wake of this devil's caper

A crimson flame washing over me

My still beating heart betwixt his fingers

Eyes alight with malicious intent

His lips pull back in a sneer

Teeth stained red with my blood

Tears choke my every breath

As my lungs catch fire

I burn

I have found myself immersed

Drenched in a perpetual desolation

Amidst the aftermath of this savage nightmare

It clings to my skin

A viscous shell

Sticky and thick

The roots burrow beneath my flesh

Deep into my bones

Twisting through marrow

There is no way to scour this anguish from within my soul

Writhing

Submerged under an unremitting devastation

I plunge into eternal damnation

Spiraling downward

Heartbreak etched inside my veins

A virus devouring heart and mind

I am exiled to impetuous insignificance

Forgotten amongst the smoldering embers of the dead

Dreams scatter about as I choke on their ashen remains

Tarnished and rusted

They disintegrate

Dust sifting between thin fingers

Tears skittering down waxen cheeks

Who will save me now?

Now that I am vanquished

Beneath the false professions

Of a duplicitous love

The deep timber of your voice

Echoes in the air around me

Your words are dissonant

Scattering about haphazardly

A cacophony rhythm

Bursting through my ears

Stumbling inside my head

A jumbled mess

My mind won't accept their meaning

But my heart tears open in my chest

You found me

Shattered

Raw

Starving for love

I craved the promises you made

But every word was a pelt against my psyche

Every touch reopened the scars left by those before

Ravenous and in ruin

Your name blisters like acid on my tongue

As I choke on the lies you fed me

Breath impales

Ripping through my lungs

My chest

Split open

Exposing the erratic beats of my fractured heart

I drink down each new second that drains from this devastation

Poison seeping into every crevice your lies cut through me

As I bathe in the flames of your treachery

A vile confession branding this anguish to my psyche

Searing it

Deep within my core

The accusations are bitter upon my lips

Thick and rancid

Strangling my voice

I never believed you would be the one

The one who left me drowning

Suffocating beneath the mire of a heinous game

Velvet petals stained in scarlet

Crimson tears upon my cheeks

Drain me into oblivion

Your thorns cut far too deep

My soul alight in agony

From loves untimely end

Withered amongst the briars

Heart bled empty from within

There is no heaven in heartbreak

No floating amongst billowing clouds

No frolicking through emerald fields

Too exhausting to love me

You said

Unworthy of even a moment

As your words grow ever distant

Disappearing into a faded memory

The price for your callous disregard

Was my soul

Thoughts drowning in murky depths

Underwater grave swallowing me whole

A cough bubbles from my lips

The weight of my sorrow

Dragging me further into a blackened abyss of memory

Time once whole

Now shattered

Sucked under by a riptide of tears

I am submerged

Into oblivion

Visions swirling inside my head

Of dreams long ago extinct

Amorphous shadows clouding sight

Of screams ever indistinct

Beleaguered moments of solitude

Amplified by souls asunder

A deluge of empty promises

Heart abandoned to vicious plunder

You loved me

Just enough

To make me crave you

A taste

A tiny sample

Then you left me

Ravenous

Love whispered from your lips

Claiming me as yours

Promises of forever

Infinite

Eternity

Through this life and every life after

To keep me by your side

But you were feeding me placebos

Keeping me placated

To absolve yourself of guilt

Aware you were too weak

Running from what is real

Too exhausted to love me

Too afraid of something true

You have the luxury of dissociating

But I feel every word

Every silence

Every echo

Of what you were too terrified to hold

It reverberates through my bones

Bleeds within my soul

You were too much of a coward to love me

And I am too broken to let go

If I sprouted wings

And flew up into the heavens

Forever out of reach

Would you finally love me?

Winter's chill seeps into my bones

Frigid

Blistering

It comes in waves

Waves of silence

Waves of disquiet

Waves of heartbreak

Tears frozen upon my cheeks

Anguish laced throughout the fabric of my soul

Woven into every cell

Breath crystallizing within my lungs

As the ariose rhythm of my heartbeat

Slows to a tenor and stalled conclusion

You loved me once

Under a diaphanous moon

Shrouded in secrecy where no one would see

Afraid to dive in

Afraid to let go

Afraid to be

A gossamer dream disintegrating from my mind

You disappeared

Left me

A severed nexus drowning in my sorrow

Cold

Numb

Your voice slides over my body

A thick shellac coating

I am helpless to scrub away

I claw at my skin

Desperate to peel off

The layers of anguish

Your touch has left behind

Hot breath at my ear

Searing hand against my chest

I am branded

Destroyed

Left in ruin

I admit nothing

Because I already handed you everything

Willingly

Without hesitation

Pretty words of saccharine charm and empty promise

Concealing cyanide deceptions

How foolish I was to love you

You don't deserve to know the level of broken you have left me in

Shattered

The pieces scattering across this crystal floor

Every step cracks

Splintering beneath my unsteady feet

Each breath sends me closer to the edge

Your voice

A haunting reverberation pulsing within my core

As the glass beneath me shivers

Ice exploding inside my chest

I fall

Spiraling into an empty oblivion

Waiting for my tears

To pierce me at the bottom

Anodyne to so many around her

Yet no one to alleviate

The weight of the sorrow

She is buried beneath

Consumed by a tempestuous life

Carving and slicing away massive portions of her soul

She wishes for numbness

But her heart doesn't beat that way

Flesh and fire

Scorching through shadow and bone

As blood rains like ash around me

A whisper of breath between blistering lips

Embers igniting within my soul

Flame and light

Beguiled between heaven and hell

A precarious balance of fate and desire

Begging for exiguous repose

Incendiary visions

Of life and love

Made whole

For a brief moment

It was mine

The truth

Mangled beyond recognition

Bloody and broken

On the tip of my tongue

I swallowed it down

The vile and bitter taste

Like acid

Scorching a trail of anguish

Eating away at my insides

Stealing the breath from my lungs

Regret

Innocence stolen a lifetime ago

Disguised as love and promise

Vicious words from an ugly heart

Encased solidly around a fragile psyche

Shackled and bound

Chipped away piece by piece

The desire to escape wanes

Time holds captive

The fragmented souls

Of the defeated

He was a fear from her past

A moment in time

Suspended within a twisted oblivion

A violent kiss on a moonless night

Razor sharp claws slicing through tender flesh

Holding her prisoner

In a life unrequited

He was only a fear

Feeding off her anguish

Savoring her demise

Beauty ethereal

Manners of utmost eloquence

An elaborate show for the world around her

Brave façade

But behind the mask she wears

Demons ravage her soul

Crimson heartbreak

Craving one who understands her

Aching for an end to the tumult within her soul

Alone she resides

Life stolen

Love fallen into darkness

Blinded by your own delusions

Afraid to let me love you

Terrified to let me near

Disappearing into the æther and unknown

I watch through veiled shadows

Of dream's unfathomable light

Alone in a hell of your design

No one left to love

Nothing left to cherish

Suspended in a moment

That will never come

You wanted me

Loved me

In silence

Hidden away behind lock and key

Invisible

A secret

A prisoner of your perfidious promises

My heart faltering within my chest

My soul shrouded beneath uncertainty

You left me incomplete

A shell of existence

In a world that no longer makes sense

Crumbling into ruin

Alone

Sacrificed dreams

My own life on hold

A pretty face to have at his side

Smile firmly in place

Masking the pain

Showy display for all to see

Only the walls would witness the truth

Behind closed doors

I was nothing more than the pedestal

He used to raise himself up

Shadows dance across the room

Dim light

Filtering through the window

Around the silhouette of a lone pigeon

The grey backdrop is eerie

I curl on my side

Squeezing my eyes shut

Your pillow lies cold next to me

A hollow numbness seeps into my veins

Emptiness

Heavy within my heart

My heart bleeds silent tears

A crimson trail of anguish and loss

Trickling over broken and bruised flesh

A voice in the distance

The words unintelligible

The cadence raw with fury

Heart wrenching in their plea

I struggle for breath

As my vision blurs with unshed tears

A touch

Feather light against my cheek

A whisper of longing in my ear

Heat envelops me

Burning a fiery path across my skin

I cling to it

Grasping for life

For a love that was never there

Waves crash against the rocks below

Jagged edges slicing through the breaker

I stand on the promontory

Wind whipping through silken tresses

Tears staining cheeks

Lips trembling with unsaid goodbyes

My heart

Flayed open in my chest

Your face

A ghostly halo before me

Within the murky depths

Of this tangled nightmare

I see you

Unearthed from beneath memories carved of stone

Fractured remnants of hope crumble around me

The ash clinging to my skin

Strangling each breath

I am a ghost to this existence

A hollow skeleton of sorrow dripping from vacant eyes

Reduced to an empty shell by your insidious promises

I never meant to love you

Never meant to hand you my heart

But you stole them both

With venom tipped fangs at my throat

Draining my soul

Remiss of consequence

Who will I be now?

When dawn breaks free from night

When my eyes flutter open

Blind to the beauty of this life

A haunted melody filters through the air

Emanating from the antiquated gramophone

The crescendo builds

Pulsing as though alive

It twists fervently

As my heart quickens to match the rhythm

Your hand brushes my cheek

My breath catches

When I open my eyes

I am alone

Midnight terror swells across my mind

A darkness pouring into every crevice

Surging waves crash against the frailty of my psyche

An overflowing deluge of regret

I am helpless to bail

Drowning in my misery

You revel my demise

Bloody and broken on the bathroom floor

Rage scorches into my flesh

Body heaving

Wracked with tears

As vitriol spills from your gaping maw

Frigid tile bites into my naked skin

As daggers rain down upon me

Piercing my mind

Slicing open my heart

How can this be what love is?

Forged within a dying nebula

Celestial light pulses through my veins

A silhouette

Invisible amongst the luminescence

A bleeding supernova

Thrumming unsteadily within my chest

I am a star without a home

Alone

Floating across an endless space

Waiting to be seen

To be loved

You made me freeze

Mid-step

Mid-breath

Mid-heartbeat

A lucid dream

Materialized from the twilight of a faltering mind

Past evanesced

Beneath a gravestone of vanished horizons

You were a collision of trespass

A blinding coalescence of tenebrous pervasion

Emitting a deafening silence

Stripping heart from soul

A haunted future awaits me

Shadowed by the darkness of a sun who refuses to shine

Behold this hell of your creation

Where desolation cheers demise

Where the tears of abandoned ghosts

Paralyze the stars

Splintered cracked

Tremors deep within

Shivering flesh

Unforgiving sin

Ice in veins

Shattered and raw

Heart flayed open

Last breath draw

Your tail lights cast an eerie glow

A crimson reflection

Like shimmering pools of blood along the darkened street

I stand torpid

As rain cascades down my body in rivulets

Your goodbye echoes into the night

Slicing across my heart

Who am I?

If I am no longer yours

The chaos of my existence

In oblivion I drown

Taunted by a hidden smile

The accusations in your gaze

A love forever out of reach

I am undeserving

A vile wretch

As I crawl through the bowels

In this hell of my own making

Maybe you were right

Maybe I deserve to burn forever

Of flesh and fire

As winter freeze scorched across the earth

Of flesh and desire

As innocence stolen by wicked mirth

Mind closed

Body numbed

As the demons converged and consumed me

He left me

Alone

Broken

Drowning in crimson and ice

A shell of existence

Forever undone

The world falls to ruin around me

As heaven crashes down to earth from above

The bang of your existence

Extinguished

A voice bleeding out from my shattered soul

Silent tears stream down my cheeks

As thorns pierce through tender flesh

Butterfly kisses

Muted halo

Sweet agony

I watch

As the leaves turn brittle and dry

Falling from the tree outside my window

The cold desolate earth swallows them up

As my heart withers away

A thick layer of ice grows within me

Suffocating my resolve to live

In ruin

How do I survive?

When my soul died with you

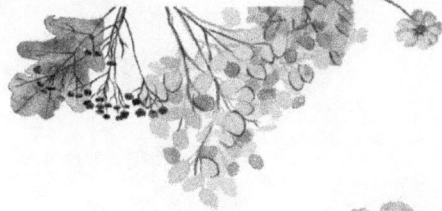

fire blazing

scorching veins

skin too tight

leaden chains

demons crying

warring within

head too loud

unforgiving sin

river of tears

down ashen cheek

heavy handed

growing weak

fluttering wings

begging for peace

feather soft kiss

sweet release

Through diaphanous dreams she wanders

Veiled beneath the shadows of an iridescent night

Haunting his memories

A ghost

An angel

An ethereal beauty burning within his veins

He feels her through every inch of his soul

An ache

Deep within the marrow of his bones

Every breath filtering from his lips

Whispers her name

Every hollow thud of his shattered heart

Beats in time with hers

In the stillness of silence

In the solace of sorrow

Waiting for the dawn

Your voice wraps over me through darkness

Visions spun of gold and light

So vivid and alive

As though I could reach out and touch you

But you drift along the periphery

Isolated

Unobtainable

An ache deep within my chest

My heart alight with longing

I awaken in tears

Dreams are beguiling that way

Endless amethyst glow

Amongst swirling emerald dreams

Alone

I wander

A lupine meadow

Whispers of what never was

Silent in my ear

Silken petals caress my fingertips

The scent of sugary sweetness

I drown

Forever wondering

What could have been

Tempestuous waters beneath me

Ominous clouds in the sky above

Churning a whirlpool of misery

Heartbreak raining from broken love

I cling to the edges of sanity

Agony batters and beats at my hull

A loss so unbearable envelopes me

Into the darkness a mournful pull

Capsized I'm thrown 'neath the surface

Sucking in mouthfuls of salt laced tears

Choking on the destruction of purpose

Consumed by my heart wrenching fears

A kaleidoscope of memory surrounds me

Blurring into a hazy fog

Haunted by the spirit of my hopelessness

Buried by the weight of my choices

Tears choke every breath

A desperate plea for redemption

Abandoned in my anguish

Grasping for a lifeline in which to cling

She will never be...

Massive

Grotesque

Vanquished

Cowering and alone

Chased by a darkness unseen

Emptiness washes over her

Freezing her skin

Turning the blood in her veins to ice

Fear consumes her mind

Every thought frantic

As the demons surround her

Muted cries rip from her throat

Scratching and clawing

Through lips raw and cracked

A scarlet trail disappearing into the night

Heart ripped from her chest as they feast

Flesh and bone

Her agony keeps them whole

Her anguish leaves them thirsting for more

There are nights

Nights when the words reverberating through my head are so piercing

I wonder how the world around me remains oblivious to the screams

Wonder how I arrived in this place

This place where silence swallows every heartbeat

A silence

So deafening in its anguish

It shatters through the darkness

An insidious shrieking

A quiddity of malevolence

Festering within my soul

A living breathing entity

Feeding off my agony

I hover

On the periphery of lucidity

On the edge of sanity

My body

Vibrating with malicious adventure

I beg for release

For the demons who haunt me

To free me from this hell

False atonement bled from your lips

Expiation I accepted as verity

Blind to the deception entwined within your desolate soul

Vile and malicious intentions

Veiled beneath lilies and lace

I clung to you

A lifeline

Unaware of the venom seeping from your pores

Infecting every breath

Left suffocating

Strangled by ostensible love

As blood rained down from the heavens

And I drowned beneath your malfeasance

The cup was smaller than it seemed

Smaller than I remembered

Once upon a time it held all my tears

Now

Now there are too many to count

Too many to measure nicely

Within the confines of such an inadequate space

They burst from my eyes

Boundless

Unceasing

As I beg for their surrender

Swiping at them fervently with unsteady fingers

Failing miserably to jockey them into submission

They pour across the barricade of my lashes

Leaving a salty trail of heartbreak scorching atop my cheeks

The admission of your guilt

An omission of the heart left bleeding between your fingers

I thought I could escape you

But the nightmares are rampant

Stifling each breath

I press against the glass

Thin and fragile

Desperate for the fresh air beyond

As if opening a window was enough

She sold her soul into darkness

When the sun rejected her light

Immured within a prison of words

Void of meaning

Empty of restraint

Swallowed down into the bowels of hellish servitude

She is cursed

For all eternity

Drowning beneath the desecration of a sacrifice surrendered

Abandoned in her torment

Her heart shattering within her chest

She will pay for his sins with blood and bone

On knees broken and bruised

As the world spins endlessly around her

Oblivious to her demise

Blind to his treacherous illusion

A maelstrom inside my head

Every word

Every promise

Every you

I leap like a frog across the lily pads

Uncertain of the danger lurking in the dark waters below

If I dive in now

Will your demons drag me under?

Will they steal the last breath from my lungs?

Will I drown?

She scolded me this morning

The little wren outside my window

Chattering angrily through the gloomy pane

My limbs

Leaden weights

Bound to a bed of sorrow

Tear stained pillow beneath my head

The world turned upside down

Heart wrenched from within my chest

Obliterated by a loss so powerful

It shattered across every fiber of my soul

Craving oblivion

Begging to disappear with you

She stared at me

As though tasting the anguish

Suffocating throughout the room

Tilted head

Obsidian eyes

Flutter of wings

She vanished

The emptiness left splintering within

I wear your silence

A thick layer of sorrow

Shrouded within my heartbreak

A deafening roar

Piercing the vulgar solitude of this unrest

I didn't realize it could hurt like this

A bittersweet amble of poison

Enveloping every cell

Coating muscle and sinew

It tethers to my psyche

A heavy film of anguish

Choking every precious breath

Moments of quiet lay forgotten

Shattered beneath the aftermath of a decimation

So powerful

It scurries across my flesh

Burrowing into the bone underneath

Seconds

Minutes

Lifetimes wasted

An irreplaceable pearl of time arranged before us

Squandered to the terror of abandoned forgiveness

I stand on the ledge

On the precipice

Between the clear life I crave

And the eradication of my spirit from your retreat

Ready to freefall

Unsure if you'll be there

To catch me at the bottom

Only a shift

Whispering across every inch of my body

Seeping into my bones

Electrifying flesh long absent of touch

Lips

Breath

A dream I never want to wake from

A fire igniting within my soul

A delicious agony devouring thought and senses

I feel you everywhere

Nowhere

No one knew

The depths of your rage

Outsiders looking in

No one knew

The hatred in your heart

An unforgiving sin

Smile painted across my face

Torrential heartache within my soul

A shell of spurious contentment

Masking the erosion of control

I deserve an Oscar for that performance

Have I been so wicked?

Punished for crimes I hold no recollection of

Transgressions from a past life

Demons rouse within my soul

I beg for repentance

For absolution I may not deserve

Despair burns through me as I cry out

Pleading for forgiveness

My only answer

Your silence

Where the weeping willows break

Beyond the emerald fields aglow

I lost you

The cerulean pond

Quiet and calm

Where we used to play as children

Haunted laughter billows on the breeze around me

The egrets alight

The whippoorwills cry

Waiting

For your heart to return

Silence

When all the words written on this page

Seem to lose their rhyme

And all the pages of memories

Have turned yellow and aged from time

A broken mind trapped in disarray

Frail in disrepair

Sucked beneath a tidal wave

Of a past who never cared

Void of reality

To time constrained

In the end

Not even hope remained

A scream rips from my throat

Sharp and jagged

Lacerating tender flesh

Raw and bloody lips

Secreting a mournful cry of heartache and redemption

Swallowed down by darkness

Heart

A rapid vibration within my body

A devastating cry of loneliness and sorrow

Devouring flesh and soul

She scratches outside my window

An ominous clatter against the shutters

Fear snakes across my spine

Burrowing into my psyche

Rising

I go

Through gossamer drapes

A ghostly image painted across frigid glass

My reflection

A banshee

Unworthy of love

Forever alone

Weeping her anguish

I remember your words

Cold winter nights sitting by the fire

Tales of evermore floating from your lips

Curling up by your side

Soaking in your heat

I remember your kindness

Spring in the air

Flowers in bloom

Holding my hand along the path by the stream

I remember your patience

Like a warm summer breeze

Blowing loose tendrils round my cheeks

Sweet kisses tickling along my neck

I remember heartbreak

Autumn leaves cascading from the trees

A dying light

Tears blinding my vision

I remember the end...

I remember your love

Drowning beneath the shadows of unshed tears

As the stars bleed across the night

A fissure splinters within my soul

Jagged and raw

Consuming every heartbeat

Silence crashes against me in waves of anguish

Loneliness haunting every ragged breath that fills my lungs

As the weight of surrender threatens to pull me under

I relax into the acquiescence of your abandon

Let the demons devour my mind

As a fever catches within my bones

I disappear into the abyss

Where the earth and the sky collide

A moment of weakness

As the walls moldered down

When my skin was too tight

And my head was too loud

A stranger to this body

A prisoner of this life

Pretty words laced with venom

And a heart thronged with ice

No feasible escape

From your insidious springe

With malevolent intentions

My soul to unhinge

When tenebrous whispers

From discordance abound

What was there to think of?

All I had to do... was drown

Whispered ghosts of a freckled past

Branded across hollowed heart

Ambrosian memories of an absent mind

Eviscerated before they could start

A severed connection of souls entwined

Stolen by times embrace

Wondering aimless through nebulous thoughts

Ephemeral existence encase

You were the catalyst of consequence

Tearing into flesh and bone

Simmering beneath desecrated sinew

Ions thick within the atmosphere

I choke on the oxygen igniting my lungs

Scorching through my body

Insidious decimation from love's nefarious design

I fall

Over the edge of sanity

Swallowed down into the darkened abyss of hell

Drowning amidst a deluge of tears

Begging for a respite

Forever abandoned

Blood turns to ice in my veins

Jagged shards

Slicing from the inside out

It tears through flesh and sinew

Carving out the raw and open pieces of my heart

His name

A ragged breath from between my lips

My mind

An indomitable prison

I beg for death's repose

She sits on the window ledge

Staring at the warmth within

Feathers wet and tattered

Storm crashing down around her

A little white dove

Tiny in her existence

Weakened by a torrential downpour

Rain soaks into her bones

Drowning the pureness of her heart

She struggles to stay upright

Against the raging winds who would steal her soul

Battered by the world

Abandoned by love

Her battle is lost

Tumbling down to the muddy earth below

She waits for an end

Fearing it will never come

Sleek muscle and sinew

Silent

Calculating

She prowls through the darkness

Eyes aglow

A dangerous beauty on the hunt

A creature of the night

Unafraid

What I wouldn't give to be her

Lady ocelot

Instead

I cower beneath you

As you wield your power over me

As silent tears stream down cheeks red and raw

I am the prey to your hunter

Closing my eyes

I wait

For courage

For strength

For my moment

To run

I stare out the window

Eyes unfocused

The landscape blurring past

A mixture of browns and greens

A splash of vibrance flashing in and out

How did I get here?

To this point

Racing from the past

Towards an unknown horizon

Slamming on the breaks

Dust billows out behind me

I jump from the car

Breath heaving in and out of my lungs

Scalding tears leave a salty trail down my cheeks

And then I see her

A ghostly entity

She eyes me wearily

A knowing within the depths of her obsidian orbs

The weight in my chest

Too heavy for my mind to hold

She meets my gaze

And I know she feels it

The emptiness of never being seen

His dark gaze bores into me

Deep into my soul

It whispers promises of passion and desire

Nerves flutter through my chest

My breath comes in short quick gasps

His fingers brush silky tendrils behind my ear

My eyes close

This flirtation with death will be my undoing

Through faded dreams I wander

A life of muted colors I fall apart

Heart barren behind shattered ribs

Eyes vacant behind crimson stare

I wait for you still

Touch

Absent

Eternal

A ghostly kiss across dying flesh

Whispers of everywhere and nowhere

Of beginning

And forever end

Twisting through madness

Clinging to ruin

I watch my life shatter before me

A fiery massacre of memories

Overflowing from the cave within my mind

Inside out and upside down

My heart

A vile wasteland of misery

Fighting for each breath

Begging for an end

Thriving in despair

Lost for a moment

Under a scarlet moon

Beneath a bleeding heart of memories

The ambrosia of forever

Now rancid upon my tongue

I choke on empty promises of yesterday

As the sky opens up

And a deluge pours down

Soaking into my bones

A tempestuous awakening within my soul

You were death

To the fragile sense of peace

To the last thread left stitched within my soul

Crashing against my existence

Breaking against my shore

Leaving me drowning in the wake of your retreat

With every new approach

Anticipation surges beneath my skin

As the heat of our bodies collide

A maelstrom of desire

Blaring within my mind

The world around me exploding into oblivion

I lie in the aftermath

Buried beneath the destruction of my own making

Staring out into the emptiness

Disappearing into the deep

With one final heartbeat

The night relaxes into silence

You offered no excuse

As you set my love ablaze

Left me choking on the ashes

As I drown beneath the flames

A stitch within the universe

My soul on the other side

As darkness falls from stars

And shadows swallow night

Emptiness consumes

My splintered bleeding heart

Ice surges through my veins

Burning tears like wildfire

Scorching across my skin

Flayed open and undone

Anguish laid to ruin

With midnight's rising sun

Familiar girl

I did not know

When I saw you in the mirror that morning

The trepidation in your eyes

Would be a foreshadowing of the heartbreak yet to come

A week of haunted silence

My heartbeat slowing

My breath growing shallow

The hollow ache within my chest

A cavernous echo of what I knew to be true

It was a quiet burning

Tingling beneath flesh and sinew

I sat alone

Waiting

Watching

As the last petal drifted to the floor

No longer a beautiful flower

Thorns cutting deep

Injecting the poison of his lie straight into my soul

Foolish girl that I am

It was silly of me to believe

When safe and sound burn to the ground

And the world goes up in flames

When heartbreak shatters through flesh and bone

And silence alone remains

An empty soul wrenched from verity

To life's impetuous end

The ghost of love's sanguine caress

Left me broken, bleeding, barren

Words whispered across my skin

Breath soft against my ear

Disappearing into the æther

As dreams fading

Slipping from mind's grasp

Into skeletal remains

An evening lost

To the coruscating dichotomy of life and love

Awake

Though not

I hold you

A memory

Tightly within my soul

Disconsolate

Begging

Through severed nexus

For one last moment

To be yours

Skin taut over jagged bones

Ravaged by your false love

I suffocate

Under the weight of my empty heart

Every cell

Consumed by the anguish you inflicted

A numbness seeps into my pores

Crystallizing inside my veins

You secured the dynamite

I light the fuse and atomize

There is a macabre rhythm

Within this ephemeral existence

An ebb and flow of time and tide

As hearts pump blood through withering veins

And souls cry frozen tears upon the desert sands

I am chained to this life

Bound to the dissonance of an eviscerated mind

A quiddity of forever

Bleeding silent pleas

From lips

Left empty and want

Demons of you

An ophidian coil

Wrap tightly around my heart

Every breath strangles my fragile sanity

My mind

A maelstrom of the torment you inflict

With your false proclamations of love

Vision blurring

Struggling for sight

For a glimpse of somewhere solid

To rest my aching soul

But all I see

Are the narrow slits of your eyes

And your gaping jaw

Lost

A tiny speck of dust

Spiraling endlessly within a ghostly luminescence

A prisoner of my sins

I cry out into the empty void

My voice a distant echo in this forgotten space

Alone

Unworthy

Left to my own ruination

In the churning nebula

Of my shattered heart

Dandelion dreams

Dance along the breeze of unconscious thought

Flittering through fingers outstretched

Grasping

I chase after you

Pace

No more than a walk

Feet struggling

Locked in slow motion

Mind swirls

Heart

An echo of undone hope

Distance grows

Out of reach

Away

Of sable shadows silhouette

Haunting dreams of hearts revoked

I lie beneath the hurricane of sibilant tears

As the sharp hiss of lover's lips pierces silent capitulations

Bleach white bones of forgotten promises surround me

Bleeding darkened tales of your mind succumbed to heartache

I am the chronicler of your anguish

I wear it

Emblazoned

Etched upon my skin

An intricately woven canvas of every breaking consequence

I disappear within the ebb and flow of your embattled disposition

Between a life laid in ruin and one yet to grasp

A tidal wave of turmoil

Leaving me drowning in your wake

She begs me to save you

Pleading from beyond

As I am buried in the aftermath

Of this soul wrenching demise

Of the only love

I have ever chosen

For myself

Of Healing

Anguish

Of love lost

Won't always

Blister

Across my skin

She slept in the garden
Beneath twinkling stars
With a handful of wishes
And a heart carved with scars

Every breath was a whisper
Every dream a dark curse
From hope's wilted kisses
Her heart beats in reverse

The roses bleed dewdrops
Whilst the lilies doth wail
Illusions are shattered
By love's unbidden fail

He watches from shadows
Hunter feasting on prey
In this gruesome adventure
In this hell she will stay

Until darkness above
Evanesces to dawn
And the light in her soul
Incandesces upon

An opalescent hope
Iridescently glows
As solace emerges
From her demons' repose

I lost myself

Somewhere

Somewhere in a life where I didn't belong

Somewhere amongst the thorns and brambles of a lonely love

I lost myself

A lifetime ago

A lifetime of being molded and branded

By those who claimed to love me

But never truly saw who I was

Was I ever even me?

I don't recognize the face of the woman in the mirror

Sharp angles

Pale skin

A spray of honeyed freckles scattered about

Eyes untrusting

Aged a thousand years

By a hurt

So deep

It nearly broke her

How did I become her?

And how do I become myself?

Now that I am free

I kiss him

As though my entire life

Depends

On this one

Single moment

In time

And perhaps

Maybe

It does

The pages of my story are crimson

Words bleeding from within my soul

Smeared by the strangling hands of those who read me prior

Tattered

Worn

Your fingers trail across my spine

Caress my fragile heart within

You read through the anguish

See the beauty inside

Bindings anew

Staring into the blackened gaze of fractured dreams

The reason to bleed grows obsolete

Blistering heartache surging within my veins

A thick Bordeaux

Flowing endlessly

From scars carved open by the dull blade of life's breaking tide

As memories refuse to accord reprieve

My soul lies vanquished beneath the umber ruins of a strangled percipience

Each imperfect breath suffocating the next

Numbness settles into the confines of my empty heart

Sinking into the hollowed surface of desolation

I welcome the hell of my vindication

Soul asunder

The weight I carry

Draped heavily atop my shoulders

A cross and titulus at my own crucifixion

Bleeding me dry

Draining me into oblivion

I hike to the edge of eternity

Mesmerized by the infinite vastness before me

My heart is all that remains

A staccato rhythm

Still beating within my chest

Refusing to acquiesce

This life has passed

Bittersweet in its surrender

As the tide of anguish breaks

As the waves push back against my tears

Dreams of an iridescent light crash through me

I am dauntless

Indomitable

Unafraid

Watching from the pyre

Fire ignites within my soul

She is there

My doppelgänger

Me

Yet not

Living the life I crave

She wears bravely

The parts of my heart

I was too afraid to show

Parts I kept hidden

Even from myself

I will burn for her sins

She will thrive from mine

It was subtle

At first

You wouldn't have noticed

The wearing thin of time across my shoulders

A shift of focus in the furrow of my brow

Delayed breath filtering from my lungs

Stuttered heartbeat burning within my chest

A change

Irreversible

Unseen

Until it was too late

One dose was too much

Until a dozen more followed

An endless cycle forcing me under

Suffocating

Tearing me down

Obliterating my fragile thread of existence

Slipping through fingers weakened from time long stolen

Empty my soul

Lay down my heart

Wash your breath over me

Mind drowning

Memories carved into flesh

A map of destruction connects the pieces of her shattered soul

History on repeat

A broken record skipping through time

Static courses through her veins

Forever chained within her own demise

In the distance

Nearly within reach

A savior

She sits

Staring out into the fading twilight

Watching as the first star blinks into existence

Life spread out before her

A universe filled with endless possibilities

Running from a past

Left buried beneath the rubble of a broken dream

Running towards a future

An unknown horizon of blossoming emergence

She sits

Words whispering through my head

Malevolent illusions of love and longing

Promises and dreams from severed lips

Disappearing within the emptiness of my shattered heart

You left me in ruin

Drowning in my tears

Condemned by the insignificance of your own existence

Malediction that sent me falling over the edge of sanity

No longer safe in my own skin

But I am not the weak fragile creature you mistook me for

My soul radiates with incandescent determination

My rise will be your undoing

I have crawled

Through the bowels of hell

Survived the savage onslaught

From the demons who dwell there

But losing you...

Losing you is what finally destroyed me

I would sell my soul

To the devil himself

If he would erase

The thoughts of you

From my mind

Heart on display

Bleeding and raw

Her tears have run dry

The well of her sorrow

No longer quenching the thirst of a lifetime of anguish

She fights for every breath

A puppet no more

To the maledictions of heartbreak

Iridescent resolve surges through her veins

Fiery determination consuming every cell

Her soul sparks

Vibrating through bone and sinew

Radiating from her flesh

Palpable within the air around her

She alights behind the shadows

Breathing them to life

Tears fill my eyes

Threatening to spill across the brim of my lashes

Heartache

Thick and bitter upon my tongue

My soul

Shattered beyond recognition

But I refuse to drown in the emptiness of myself

Refuse to succumb to deaths demands

I fight

Rising anew

Devoured by darkness

I prowl through the night

Blood surging within my veins

No longer victim to the chaos of a broken life

To promises left undone from empty lips

My soul ablaze

I see you

Through crimson coated haze

The sweet taste of vengeance

Thick atop my tongue

With a valorous heart

I strike

Glasses

Shards

Splinters of a broken life

Turned upside down

Inside out

A moment of escape

A fragile sense of security

Left floating

Fluttering

Drifting away

Distant memories lost amidst broken time

Holding on to what never was

What never could be

I lost you

Loved you

Longed for you

Left you

Her heart is spun

With gold and grace

Soft melodies of love surrendered

A Symphony

Surging within her soul

Her voice

A haunting remembrance

Sorrow flowing through crystal tears

A deluge breaking against porcelain skin

She refuses to swallow the fear forced upon her

Refuses to succumb to shadowed illusions of life

Left drowning...

Empowered

She finds the strength

To survive

The ink is not yet dry atop the page

When the tears begin to flow

Crystal drops of glistening surrender

They rain down upon my sins

Staining the fibers

Smearing the words

As my vision blurs

As my soul is cleansed

A celebration of sorts

Though not

Perhaps death would be a more apt description

Is there a difference?

When one life ends and another begins

A bittersweet Symphony of past and future

Colliding within the equivocating present

A wasted lifetime

An infinite possibility

When the earth falls from beneath unsteady feet

And the world burns to the ground around me

I grasp for something solid to cling to

Succumbing to the ethereal hope

Of the unknown

The charred remnants

Of my still beating heart

Crumble between your fingers

Wandering amongst the shards of an inescapable sorrow

I am lost to the moments forgotten by time

Held captive by a whispered promise of forever

I stumble

The jagged edges of my anguish

Biting deep gashes into tender flesh

Palms dripping bloody tears

Staining the ground beneath me

Scarlet petals across a barren landscape

I push myself forward

Despite the demons clawing at my heels

Despite the overwhelming urge to succumb

I push myself forward...

And rise

The pieces float around me

Dust

Scattering in the breeze

Tiny

Inconsequential moments of our life together

Empty and abandoned

Their meaning lost

Voided from within your heart

Happy to forget who I never was to you

Each one etched into my soul

A promise yesterday was too weak to hold

A promise tomorrow will be strong enough to carry

I hover in the shadows

A stranger in my own existence

Nothing more than a shell of my former self

My skin

Too tight

Stretched taut over brittle bones

Threatening to shatter under the weight of your betrayal

My mind

Too loud

A cacophony mixture of self-loathing and doubt

Crumbling my already fragile psyche

You left me to drown

In the downpour of your contempt

Left me to rot beneath the necrotizing corpse of love's demise

Somehow

I still breath

Somehow

Blood still flows through my veins

My heart still beats within my chest

And I survive

You preyed upon my brokenness

With malicious desire

Slicing across the scars

Carving open my flesh

Devouring the love from within my soul

As if it were yours alone to possess

Blatant disregard for the consequences to my heart

You left me in the wake of your satisfaction

A casualty of your vicious machinations

Buried beneath a silence only I could hear

Burning within a hell of your creation

I crawled through the flames

Clawed my way out of the ash

Found my own redemption

Reveling

In the emptiness

Of you

Douse me in gasoline

Light the match and spark the flames

Stand back

Watch me burn

Enraptured by the decimation you create

Smoke filled lungs breathe poison across my flesh

As I choke on the stench of betrayal

Biting your tongue

Pretty words bleed into my mouth

Vile manipulations

Acrid and bitter

I eat the meager remnants of your empty soul

Swallow them down to fill the hollow ache of deceit

Cheating death

Clinging to a thread

The blood in my veins turns to ash

I bury you in the past

Six feet deep

Beneath the rubble of a broken life

A skeleton of void existence

You came to me in darkness

An angel amongst the damned

A moment of fragile surrender

From heart drowning beneath the sands

Of time wrought by vicious anguish

Bleeding sorrow from open veins

Swallow me down into the embers

As my body alights in flames

Visceral desire surges

Assuaging open wounds

Heated flesh left burning

Fire designed to heal and soothe

Drinking in your final breath

Claiming it as my own

Plunging over the edge of oblivion

New life ignites within my soul

As earth and moon collide

With stars bereft of light

Obsidian afterglow

Staining soul's tumultuous plight

A moment of revelation

Drowning amidst despair

Memories painted crimson

Hearts abandoned to disrepair

Standing on the horizon

On a precipice unknown

Sweet kiss upon the emptiness

From sun's incandescent throne

Counterfeit confessions of repentance

Bleeding across my soul

Forgiveness handed freely

For absolution undeserved

Heart overflowing

With unfinished deceit

Machinations of ill intent

I exonerated your past

To appease our present

But the future belongs only to me

Ensnared in a web of deception

The blade of your malice at my throat

Piercing flesh

Dripping scarlet tears

You took my love

As the weakness of a vulnerable heart

Preyed upon my soul when it was lost and broken

Unaware of the fire simmering beneath my skin

Power churning

Demanding to be set free

You were the one who ran

While I stood my ground until the end

Pulled beneath the surface

In over my head

Silence in my mind arrogating control

Demanding reprieve

Daring me to succumb

As the waters disperse

The air heavy within my lungs

Suffocating

You clipped my wings

Feather by feather

Fettering me to your desolation

I prayed for death

But my demons wouldn't abide

Now every teardrop fuels my resolve

Every scar incites enmity for your reviled heart

I refuse to waste into an empty oblivion

Refuse to relinquish my soul

I watch

As the earth opens up

Swallowing you below

Tears rain down from the heavens

As I breathe in the petrichor

Thick within the air

I fly

I am trapped

Within this moment

In slow motion

As the world spins wildly around me

Like a sloth

I hang precariously amidst the branches of this life

My mind ablaze

Burning with a desire for something so long out of reach

My body

Frozen

Waiting

For the instant

You see me

You lured me in with your pretty words

Promises of a life I so craved

A lupine smile

Baring deadly fangs

Blind to see the beast within the man's eyes

Out of my darkness

Straight into your hell

Little did you know

I was the wolf in sheep's clothing

How do I apologize?

For letting you destroy me

For handing you the power to break my soul

I beg for mercy

Burning bridges to the past

A prisoner to my own demise

A picture frame before me

A masterpiece of tears drowning failed mistakes

Laughter bubbles from my lips

As sin spills from my tongue

A match

Flickering between trembling fingers

A vacant life

Outlined in guilt

I set it all ablaze

I savor the silence of your words

Piercing through my psyche with aphonic heartbreak

A muted Symphony only my soul has heard

Resonating beneath my skin with unrestrained anguish

Blinded by frivolous promises of an egregious mind

Naked and bare in my desolation

My heart thrums within my chest

An ariose hope of dulcet awakening

Born from a spark

Forged from the heartache of a shattered existence

A flame

Surging to life beneath the ashes of soul wrenching anguish

Fire burns within her veins

Scorching across the desolation

Feeding her determination

As fury ignites within her chest

Wrapping and molding

A living

Breathing entity

Seeping from her pores

Scarlet spills across her vision

As heat envelops her heart

Beneath her piercing gaze

New strength takes hold

She grasps for it

Refusing to surrender

You stand before me

A silhouette

Shadowed darkness

Amorphous dissimulation

I remember every promise

Every lie

Every profession of desire

Knavish words spilling from your lips

Inveigled deception to pilfer love

The venom from the heartache you precipitated

Feeding my tears

Filtering through every fiber of my being

I watch the decay

Mesmerized by the destruction

The earth falling beneath me

My soul in flames

My heart the casualty of your vile machinations

But I refuse to surrender

As a shift emanates from the universe

A light sparks within my dreams

Emerging from the emptiness

I rise from the ashes of your annihilation

A vision

A haunting nebulous of vengeance

I am the succubus scourging your nightmares

I am the regret burning through the veins

Of your mediocre existence

Silence echoes through my veins

Pumping

Rushing

From a heart surrendered to the perilous machinations of love

A mask slips into place

A direction not my own

Eviscerated

As innocence lost

A veil lifted

Recast into a role with an armored soul

A vixen I shall become

She exists within the tenebrosity of my fractured heart

A haunting vision

Etched into memories

Suspended

Beyond the ebony rigidity of every faltering beat

Reverberating through my aching bones

Exhausted

Drained from time's imposition of flesh and blood

She remains veiled

Beneath the gossamer illusions of incandescent mourning

A diaphanous dream of my soul's desire

A halo of resilience bleeding from her spirit

I crave her strength

Whispering along my fingertips

She is me...

Almost within reach

I am no longer yours

To manipulate and control

Yet

You hover on the periphery

Lying in wait

The bitter taste of your contempt

A thick coat atop my tongue

Choking the thoughts from my voice

You loathe seeing me stand on my own

But my inadequacies were only in your mind

Your demons try to break me

But mine have already won

With your fragile ego

You tore me to shreds

Kept me chained in the uncertainty of my own mind

The tattered remnants of my soul

Used as kindling

For your fire scorching out of control

Scraping and clawing

I found my way out

Marred

Maimed

Somehow still breathing

I survive

In the aftermath of a shattered tomorrow

Beyond the twilight mourning of heart's demise

An unforgiving darkness swallows me down into her nightmare

As starlight tears bleed across an obsidian sky

A petrified forever of hollow sweetness burrows into my bones

You were a mesmerizing emptiness of nevermore

A battle destined to destroy me

But there is a safe place for my demons to repose

A waking surrender for my soul to claim home

An evocation of hope sparks along the horizon

As dawn breaks free from her umbral prison

Breathing light into existence within my core

Poison fills my veins

Intimate knowledge of the harsh realities reigned upon me

Painfully aware of my own fragility

I bleed it from my heart

A crimson river

Wisdom I sculpt from time and circumstance

Words of tomorrow inscribed in ink within my soul

Surrender not

Fly free

I didn't recognize her

When the dust settled

When the tears ran dry

When the breath in my lungs grew calm

I didn't recognize her

Without the bruises

Without the scars

Without the heartache

I didn't recognize her

But I knew instantly

The woman rising from the ash

Was me

She waits

Lost amidst the shadows of sorrow

Between a life left in ruin and hope waiting to hold

A fragile thread of longing

A crimson stain of heartbreak across her soul

She waits

Lost amidst the tears of blurred promises

Between agony laid to rest and happiness fluttering within reach

A fierce spark of desire

Anticipation thrumming within her heart

She waits

I was the heart you laced with cyanide

I was the calm before your storm

I gave up everything to love you

But you drown me in your scorn

The purity in my soul

Both intrigued you and enraged

You couldn't simply love me

You had to bury me in shame

You took away my life

Made a prisoner of my mind

Years I spent in anguish

While you fed off the tears I cried

I will never go back to that place

Where my words blur across the page

I will never go back to that place

Where I no longer have a name

She watches the world around her

Weary of the pain ever hovering along the periphery

The demons of her past

Waiting for her to miss a step

Waiting to drag her under

She has seen the underbelly of hell

Far too many times before

Clawed her way free for only a moment's reprieve

Choked on the flames licking at her skin

But she refuses to give up

Refuses to let it ruin her

Even if it takes forever

She will find her way

Condemned by the agony scorching through my veins

I stare at the blaze that surrounds me

A raging inferno ignited by my own tears

A lifetime of anguish and torment leading up to this point

I cling to my sanity

Sturdy in my resolve

Not to burn down

With the flames

She slept on petals of dandelion dreams

A pocket of wishes by her side

Dancing upon the wings of a butterfly's kiss

Waiting for her heart to arrive

There were moments of poise scarred with breaking release

Faint remembrance lacking proper goodbye

Her shattered resilience strewn in pieces about

As she longed for her season to fly

An enchanted atrocity of fate's inapt design

Echoes rippling through stitches of time

She stands on the precipice of an allusion survived

Awaiting the universe to align

A spark of anger ignites inside my chest

I grasp for it

Unwilling to relent

It breathes into me

Filling my lungs with a burning need for survival

Blazing across my skin

Fiery kisses of intent

Soaking into every pore

You will see the earth scorch

Before I ever give in

I sit

Staring out across the horizon

As the sun and moon collide in the sky above me

A blinding explosion of promises undone

Of past evanesced

The world fades into darkness

A calmness seeps into my pores

Heart

Mind

Soul

A syzygy within my body

Awakening

Anew

Alive

Abandoned amongst the ashes of a scorched love

Choking on smoke and ruin

You left me

Soul laid bare

Heart split open

Drowning in silent anguish

Naked

Depleted

A fire sparks within my veins

Resolution awakening

Igniting a burning desire for vengeance

Your fate

Appendant

To my survival

When calamity echoes

Beyond the hollowed outbreak of shattered determination

Paving the path before me

With the blood of inveigled evocations

The road leading me into reprieve

Is not laced with butterscotch ribbons of sugared tears

Intricately woven between our fractured souls

My demons race behind me

Clawing at enfeebled flesh

I watch

As a piece of my heart dies

Gravity pulling it down

Into the devil's malevolent embrace

I invoke unto my absolution

Tracing the curve through unmitigated nightmares

Fraying at the seams

Waiting for your touch...

To set me free

Drowning in oblivion

Beneath a tidal wave of tears

Dragging me into the inky abyss below

A light wraps around me

A beacon in the night

Guiding the way to shore

Strength surges through flesh and bone

Renewed determination to stay afloat

Finding my way

Still lost to the deep

Desperately clinging to hope

A face materializes from the darkness

Begging me to stay

I grasp for the incandescence

For the promise of new life

For the promise

Of something

Real

Waking nightmares

Amid gossamer dreams

Quixotic delusions of macabre deception

Your face hovers within the recesses of my frayed sanity

Taunting with a forever that never was

A vision of darkness beneath velvet evisceration

Desolation behind a hollowed heart

Resilience surges beneath anguish and ruin

Sparking within my shattered soul

A vestige of silence overwhelms me

As I stare at the ghostly image in the mirror

Pallid skin

Lifeless eyes

Consumed by a deadly urge for vengeance

Retribution at the tip of my fingers

Acid eating away at my flesh

Crimson spills across my vision

Your reckoning

I become

Determination

Radiates from within her soul

A blinding luminescence

Of perseverance

She refuses to surrender

Alone in this gig

Where light and shadows blur

Where desire is a fantasy

And broken hearts have no cure

Alone in this life

Where day and night blend as one

Where love is unspoken

And black souls see no sun

Alone in this sorrow

Where agony collides

Where memories disappear

And new life resides

Words shatter across her mind

Broken memories of a forgotten tomorrow

Heartache fades into muted obsidian

Blurring yesterday into an ochre existence

A splintered melody emanates within her soul

Cerulean desire twisting into a haunting Symphony

Whispering into the æther and unknown

Waiting for her moment

Waiting for her love

To rise

Rising out of the darkness

I float endlessly thru a shimmering effervescence

Illuminated by a distant spark of incandescent wonder

Suspended between lives

Craving eternity

I refuse to cosset my fears

Refuse to assuage the unknown

My soul

Alight with longing

I fight

A crack

A fissure

Aching deep within my bones

Lips with empty sound

Choking on sorry

Forgive

And forget

Enveloped in a past of furry filled fear

I break free of the chains who have held me captive

Steady feet

Unyielding will

Wrapped in a fiery spark of love anew

I soar

You always thought you were such a gas

Jokes at my expense

Cutting me down at every turn

Vicious humor you claimed to be love

I was the clown in a relationship filled with daggers

A circus of lies under a tent of heartbreak

Now the joke is on you

I am gone

Untethered

Stripped naked

Bleeding and bare

I will never be who they say I am

Flesh exposed

Shattered bones

I will die before I let him win

Raw and beaten

Fueled by tears

I will burn the world around me

Soul asunder

Heart consumed

I will vanquish all who try to destroy me

When sleep wages an unfair battle

In a vicious game of hide and seek

And the demons chasing through maleficent nightmares

Refuse to offer the slightest repose

Staring into the darkness

I see your face

Hovering before me

A fallen angel of nefarious desire

A wickedness of insidious intent

Clawing at my skin

Bleeding my heart dry

Every word meant to impale

Every promise meant to shatter

Suffocating beneath the festering emptiness of your abandon

Twisted machinations of your broken mind

I refuse to succumb

As a light sparks in the distance

My soul ignites with fury

I will bask

In the magnificence

Of your annihilation

A lifetime

Played out in technicolor memories

Moments

Uncertain choices

Endless reel of regret

An empty void fills my chest

My heart in ruin beneath your feet

So many wasted years

In which you never truly saw who I was

Now it's too late

The movie is over

And I am free

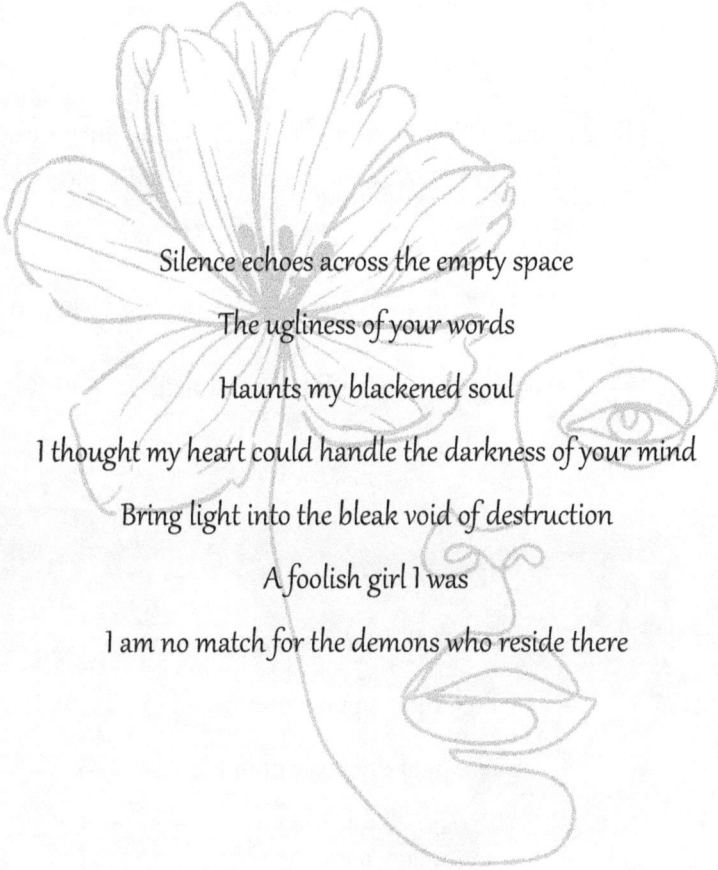

Silence echoes across the empty space

The ugliness of your words

Haunts my blackened soul

I thought my heart could handle the darkness of your mind

Bring light into the bleak void of destruction

A foolish girl I was

I am no match for the demons who reside there

Words and feelings

Flutter about my mind

Swimming through my veins

Like parrotfish gliding through a sea of crystal blue

Vibrant

Vivid

They glisten

Dashing this way and that as I watch

Silently

Envisioning

One by one I sort them

Scrawl them across paper

Etch them upon my skin

An ocean of dreams within me

Waiting to be set free

I cry

I have cried

Enough tears to drown a thousand lifetimes in

Heart wrenching anguish I have tried desperately to escape

Bruised and scarred

Bleeding and surrendered

By those who claim to love me

By those with vile intent

I run

I keep running

Until the road before me lies barren

When the life behind me smolders into a wasted oblivion

Feet raw

Soul screaming for reprieve

From a past I was helpless to control

From a future that remains hidden

I wait

I keep waiting

Heart between brittle fingers

Still beating

Searching for hope along the distant horizon

Watching as the sun and earth collide

As the world around me awakens

To a new moon

To a new day

When I am finally free...

To live

Split in two

Did you see me?

Wandering lost amongst the dandelion fields

Was I so invisible for you never to have noticed?

Wishes blowing in the breeze

Missing pieces floating out of reach

Unable to catch even one

Teardrop whispers shadowed in gossamer green

Drenched in the blood of a lifetime of lies

Unworthy and alone

You took everything

Cut my heart from my chest

Leaving an empty shell of yesterdays' mournings

Somehow

I keep breathing

Somehow

I am still alive

Mangled

Broken

A scarlet rose grows within my soul

Silken petals nourishing and filling me

Thorns carved from heart wrenching madness

Do you see me now?

Standing before you

You left me in pieces

I will make myself whole

I forgive you

For not loving me

The way you promised me you would

Excusing every lie as misunderstanding

Burying the heartache behind a fabricated smile

I was not blind

To your propensity for duplicitous inclinations

I saw them all

Veiled behind counterfeit integrity

Shadowed beneath my own earnestness for something real

Until a shiver rippled through the atmosphere

A shift heaved within my soul

Releasing my heart from your burden

Veins open

Anguish bleeding dry

I forgive myself

For ever believing

You were sincere

Worthless. Uncertain. You made me

Cut me down so you could feel tall

Shattered. Broken. Held prisoner

In a life where I was kept small

I never needed your counterfeit charity

Never needed your claims of love

Now I fight for the freedom you stole

Raining fire from the heavens above

Day draws to an end

Evening drowns into darkest night

Alone I lie in wonder

At the ferocity of my inner light

This place where I now find myself

Somewhere between my heaven and your hell

Somewhere between a shattered life of misery

And possibility I have never felt

I will credit my own strength

Despite your efforts to destroy me

Surviving here without you

In this life where I am now free

Clouds snake through the sky

Dark and ominous they writhe

Painting the moon an onyx nimbus

A thunderous cry reverberates through my bones

Blood ablaze inside my veins

Heat rolls from my body in waves

The storm above

Syntonic to the one within

As I set the world afire

A moment of hesitation

A brief interlude between numb and alive

What if?

Sour on the tip of my tongue

I stare into the vast emptiness of my life

Into the heart of the evils who have pillaged my soul

Broken

Desolate

A shell of existence

In a world where color and time have lost all meaning

No more

No more will I succumb to the madness of my own annihilation

Drifting blindly through my own downfall

Teetering on the edge of sanity

I fall

Plunging into the unknown

Possibilities galore

An end

A beginning

Alive

There was a method to your madness

A formula to your fiendish fabrications of forever

Cunning calculations of conceit

Laced with lecherous loquaciousness

Believing you could break me

Delighting in the devastation of my downfall

I would deliver my soul to the devil himself

For the benefit of observing you burn

But your egregious existence isn't worth my expiation

Karma can keep you

She will right the wrong

Requisition my revenge

My heart will heal

Finally free

Forever

I am the sea on a blackened night

Waves breaking against your rocky shore

Roiling and twisting

My surface

A constant shift of chaos and turmoil

Created by the uncertainty of your love

Far below

In the darkest depths

A dangerous calm lies in wait

A soul

Growing stronger with every turn of the tide

You fed off my pain

Devoured my agony

Left me drowning in my own tears

But I am the sea on a blackened night

I will break you with my waves

Until you see the strength

I hold within

Lost in the glow of early morn

My eyes flutter open

Hues of gold dance about the room

The uncertainty of this moment

Of love

Of loss

Of heartbreak

A beehive of self-doubt surrounds me

A static buzz incessant across my mind

I feel you everywhere

Yet nowhere

Your voice

A soft whisper in my ear

A gentle reminder of what was

What could be

What is

Stand there and look pretty

You had better know your place

Stand there and look pretty

They only need to see your face

Stand there and look pretty

No one cares what you have to say

Stand there and look pretty

Fuck you, darling... I will no longer behave

When heartbeats coalesce

Amidst the hollow wreckage of invisible anguish

A stolen kiss blurs the fingerprints of an empty past

I bury the bones

Beneath a headstone engraved by fate's bleeding light

A name

Etched within the darkness of love's repose

My sins melt

Under the pyre of secrets untold

Hidden behind a garden of crumbling stones

The scent of eternity wafts over me

The rich smell of forgotten betrayal

I fall

Swallowing the writhing tempo of forgiveness

Rewriting the history

Of an absolved forever

Rubble and ruin

Shattered soul

I walk away

Refusing to look back

Shards of my broken heart

Lay scattered at my feet

Biting into weary flesh

Sorrow filled lungs

Drowning in fiery tears

Still

I walk

Away from the desolation

On the horizon

A new light

A new heart

A new hope

Memories of a life long forgotten

Flood my mind with hurricane force

My philtrum quivers

As my lips purse tightly together

A shot of fear sends adrenaline coursing through my veins

The urge to run is overpowering

But I stand my ground

Ready to fight for this new life

Home

Did I falter?

Inside my soul

Within this place of shattered dreams

Fractured and splintered

By the emptiness of my heart's echoing destruction

Reverberating through the choking tears of a mutilated existence

Desecrated and ravaged by a distorted veracity

I am livid for the innocence lost

Stolen before I was strong enough to save myself

But I shed those vicious memories

Exuviate them like a buried end

Submerge them

Beneath a caustic pool of resurrected quintessence

I yearn for this new life

Crave the love now within reach

No longer afraid

No longer bound

To the heart wrenching madness

Of before

Terror vibrates within my veins

Pulsing through blood and sinew

My body is drained and raw

Exhausted from decades of lies and heartache

Alone I break

Desperately searching for a lifeline

For a shred of hope to grasp onto

Endlessly crawling through the bowels of hell

Clinging to my sanity by the thinnest of threads

I beg for salvation that will never come

I beg for a love too far out of reach

Closing my eyes

The tears break free

A salty trail burning across my cheeks

I beg for the end

For the earth to open up

To swallow me down into a final resting place

The demons converge

My heart stills

And then

A voice

Calling out

From the darkness

Alone and afraid I stand

Unseen by the world around me

An invisible shadow swathed in the eerie gloam

Battered and bruised by those who falsely professed their love

Darkness settles deep within my soul

Consuming all hope

The thread

Slipping through my fingers

Lost to the heart wrenching destruction of what never was

Caught between the worlds of the living and the dead

Uncertain of which way to fall

Teetering on the brink of an unknown path

I close my eyes

And I wait

I will not bail

Nor abandon

Letting the darkness suck me down

As the demons ravage and ruin me

I will be lost before I am found

A storm rages within my soul

A wicked and violent tempest

My body

Broken and mangled

My mind

Alert

On edge

Swirling in the darkness

A child

Denied love

Stolen innocence

Always left

Always lost

Time pilfered away

A woman

Craving love

Forever withheld

Always longing

Always waiting

Time passing away

A broken heart

Slowly reassembles

Glimpses love

Glimpses life

Time stands still

Horizon of hope

This life was never traditional

Though my heart endeavored to dream of such oddities

Always on the outside looking in

Through a window painted thick with time

 I am a stranger in my own existence

Irregular

Awry

My soul holds no set pattern

No conformity

I make my own

Time thrashes about

Inconsistently

Every frame dismembered

Screaming beneath thick melancholia

Sojourned behind cravings drained of excuse

I sacrificed blood and tears for secrets not my own

Delusions fueled by the scars engraved upon my soul

Out of the desolation

Out of the emptiness

I grow

From an unfinished existence

A flourish of consciousness sheltering a fragile heart

Free of the chains who have kept me bound

I feel the difference

Palpable within my bones

I am no longer simply breathing

I am alive

Of Love

As errant thoughts

Give way to madness

My love for you

Is the only certainty

I will never question

I hear your voice from the shadows

A susurrus breath against my ear

A deep cadence bleeding into my veins

Pulsing through my chest

Breathing life into existence beyond the sorrow

You hold my heart

Beating anew

In the palm of your hands

There was never a question if I would relinquish it to you

It was yours

Always

My body knew with undeniable truth

Before my mind made the conscious decision

But the tears threatening to drown us now

Are not my own

The demons converging on the fringes

Demand blood

I would sacrifice myself to save you

Scorch the earth if it meant you would be free

There is no price I won't pay

To absolve you of your anguish

Even if the budget for this heartbreak...

Is my soul

It started as an itch

A tiny scratch

Bleeding beneath the surface of my sanity

A hum

Buzzing across my skin

Twisting into an echoing wail

The decay growing and spreading

A malignant invasion of time and space

Crushing every promise

Draining light and love from existence

I grasp with weakening fingers

Bloody and raw

Trembling bones splintering

Fracturing underneath the weight of unbridled anguish

All semblance of control lies abandoned

Beyond the memories of what never was

What never could be

I will fall with you into a voided nothing

Into an unrestrained everything

If you'll let me hold you

Fade with me into this beautiful surrender

Where the damage isn't wasted

Where the scars no longer matter

A smile

Tiny

Foreign on lips long absent of sun

Unnoticeable to those around her

Nearly indiscernible even to herself

A slight curve

Visible in her being

Eyes close

Breath stalls

It was not charm

Only a simple kindness

The impact he could never fathom

On a heart lost to the current

Pulled under with the tide

Her soul beleaguered by heartache

A smile

Tiny

Reaching out through the darkness

Was it wicked of me to love you?

To hand you my heart and open my soul

I would surrender all that I am

For a single moment in time

One touch

To know

I am still alive

Hold me to your words

Promises of a life so yearned for

Bleed me from my solitude

Pneuma entwined

Now whole

I remember light and dark

The sound of your voice whispering across my skin

The honeyed scent of longing

Like potpourri

Tickling my nose

Waking my senses

Incandescent desire burning within my veins

Absent of rational thought

The touch of your body against mine

Mellifluous heartbeat thrumming within my chest

In dreams long faded

A life laid to rest beneath a deluge of tears

I remember you

My heart

My soul

My love

As memories fade to dust

Tears bleeding from the spire

Break me down into evanescent quietude

Carve the scars from within my soul

Leave them burning on the pyre

I write heartbreak into the ash

Watch as it disappears

Words of forever and always

Conflate into diaphanous murmurs of nevermore

A dalliance of purgation

An elixir of reprieve

On the other side of this life

Where the pain ends

Where the sorrow releases control

I find you

Haunt me in moments of silence

Steal the breath from within my dreams

As I lie beneath shattered illusions of the past

Of a life wasted

Heart guarded by circumstance

Your voice washes over me

Guiding me through darkness

Anchoring me to the shore

A light

Weeping amidst the shadows

Sweet effervescence

Quenching my soul

Assuaging shared secrets of heartbreak

When dawn filters in

When the nightmares remain hidden away

I never needed you to save me

But your love will make me whole

The air was stifling

Suffocating within my soul

So I opened it

A tiny crack

The window into my heart

A hesitation

A flutter of vulnerability

You were there

Slipping in so silently

A warm breeze on a summer day

A whispered kiss along my neck

There was no time to be afraid

To take a step back

You wrapped around me

A light

Invisible until now

And I finally found peace

Within your love

Could I exist outside my body?

Separate my soul from the sorrow within

Generate the perception of a heart unbroken

Using every shard and splinter

To create a juncture of consequence

To sheathe the exquisite chaos

Which lies silenced within variegated dreams

We manifest into existence an actuality

Reality unmarred

By the vicious world demanding our surrender

Clinging to one another

To the moments of quiet fervor

To the aching need

Smoothing a shared heartbreak

We breathe in the serenity

Of our love

Was it forbidden for me to love you?

Falling into a chaos

So blinding in its beauty

The world outside evanesced into an obscure obsoleteness

An obsession of souls

A redolent serenity overflowing within my veins

You are the eternal rhythm

Thrumming through the lissome threads of my every heartbeat

The quiddity of my existence

Intricately woven into the breath filling my lungs

Your name is etched across every cell of my being

Every fiber smoldering with susurrus quietude

As a whispered sigh escapes 'tween my lips

Relinquished from the sorrow breaking within my heart

Alight in this moment

Alive in the hope

Of you

I have wandered this path before

Every bend

Every curve

Whispering through emerald dreams

A melody of unfinished rhythm

A Symphony aching to crescendo

Beneath the celadon canopy of my soul's desire

Out of the shadows

Reaching for a moment

Waiting for forever

I hold my breath

My heart beating out an unrestrained tempo

The cadence of anticipation pulsing through my veins

The end has always been out of reach

Too far for my feet to carry me

Until now

Until you

My love

Lost to your touch

Fire igniting across every inch of my skin

Hot breath tickling sensitive flesh

I open to you

A deep ache within my soul

Heart thrumming wildly within my chest

Consumed by longing

Desire surges through my veins

Your name

Whispered across my lips

Your taste

Sweet on the tip of my tongue

I drown in the feeling of you

Everywhere around me

Melting

Seeping into my bones

As the world around us

Fades into oblivion

We fall

Pinion embrace

Souls rooted in junctures of heartache

There is a wuthering defiance within my bones

A pivotal tempest emerging

Desire quakes beyond the broken pieces of my vanquished heart

Your voice resonating within my psyche

An audible caress synthesizing the remnants of my shattered existence

You free me from the wreckage

Breathe into me ambrosia tears of promises renewed

Hope revived

Pulsing within my veins

Awakening my love

The world outside sits quiet and still

My heart plays a heavy staccato inside my chest

Dawn breaks across the horizon

A Symphony of crimson and gold

Filtering through gossamer drapes

I hold my breath

Waiting

Your arms wrap around me

Body flush against mine

Whispering of love

A touch felt through every inch of my soul

Though your hands have never been near me

A kiss igniting every cell ablaze

Though your lips have never been close

My heart beats with no uncertain desire

Longing only for you

For a single moment

For a lifetime

To be real

From the honeyed kisses

Of bumblebee daydreams

Through the rose-colored lenses

Of fleeting innocence

I found a moment

Of something real

In your eyes

A hollow ache deep within my soul

Emptiness

A heavy weight pressing down upon my unsteady heart

Every beat

A muted teardrop

Crimson and raw

Regrets of a life long passed

Love turned to ash

By a burn so slow

I didn't realize we were even blazing

Now light seeps in

Slowly creeping through the narrow cracks

I fight for the darkness

Terrified to let it slip from between my fingers

A piece of me for so many years

I desperately cling

Yet he chips away at the shadows

An angel of mercy

A demon sent from the fiery pits of hell

My torment

My undoing

My repentance

My love

Heart flayed open

Laid bare before you

In a ceremony of fractured souls

The weight of your scourge

Kindred to my demise

A ruptured coalescence of devotion

An extant of malicious grace

She is a vision of diminishing grief

An unattainable peace

Dancing amongst the shadows

Taunting

I ache to heal the desolation boiling within your mind

Yearn to pile every heartache

Every sorrow

Into a raging conflagration of salubrious spirit

I swallow down your anguish

As if it were my own

Feel it roiling inside me like a turbulent wind

I will keep her safe

Until the agony can no longer hurt you

I will love you into eternity

If you'll only let me in

Erratic heart

A staccato rhythm inside my head

A maniac of vibrations within my chest

Blood rushing through veins

Fire scorching across flesh

A touch

A taste

A longing so deep it's carved across every fiber of my existence

Your lips against mine

Body pressed close

I melt into you

Until the only sound left

Is your heart

Beating in tune

With mine

Fingers trace the bow of my lips

The shallow groove of my philtrum

Eyes closed

Whispered sigh

Shivers break across my skin

A soft touch cupping my cheek

Heat of breath

Smooth lips against my own

Gentle

Yet urgent

Heart thrumming in my chest

Love's first kiss

Desecrated

Left in ruin

Seized by the savage maelstrom of a life laid to waste

Winds crash about

As I beg for reprieve

Helpless to stay upright

Splintering

Shattering

Bare

You grasp for me

Clutching the pieces of my broken heart

Anchoring me to your soul

Hold me now unto forever

Keep me rooted in your love

Eternity unyielding

I thought I was immune to your fractious proclamations

But they cut into me

Slicing through flesh and sinew

Sawing into the bone beneath

Weapons of virulent lips

Malevolent contempt for the purity you found sheathed inside my soul

You wrenched me under

Strangling me beneath the darkness

But I found a light sparking within my vanquish

A lucent hope far beyond your reach

Enveloping love

Infusing my heart

With new life

Sweet persimmon heartbeats

Thrumming within her soul

Igniting obsidian memories

With teardrops of refined gold

Entwined beneath the canopy

Of soothing ambrosial haste

She finds a home within the light

Of loves unwavering embrace

There are thoughts

Heavy within my veins

Leaden and cumbersome

They choke my heart

Each beat struggling for a rhythm

An unfamiliar staccato

Disjointed and abrupt

Pouring from my chest

There is no melody left to placate my soul

To render the emptiness

Tearing apart the frayed edges of my consciousness

There is only time

Marred by the stillness of an absence waiting to pervade

Awakened by a touch

By the deep cadence

Of soft-spoken words

Of new love

My heart is flayed open

Everything inside of me

Raw and bloody

You sift through my sorrow

My agony

Sort out the salvageable pieces

The heady taste of your words

Lingers on my tongue

So potent

I might drown in it

So intoxicating

My soul surrenders

And I succumb

Amidst the wreckage of an obliterated life

Amongst the ashes of a soul stretched thin

A pilfered heart left bleeding and raw

You saw me

Beyond the agony

Behind the scars

Beneath the broken

You drank in my tears

As though they were vital to your own existence

Kissed away the anguish scorching across my flesh

 Gentle words whispered into the darkness

Beckoning me into your light

Without thought

Without hesitation

I fell

It was never work to love you

All I had to do...

Was breathe

A mask

A façade

Veiling heartbreak from the world

Pale lips stretched taut

Paper thin

She grasped for it

In moments of sorrow

In moments of surrender

A dam to ebb the flow of tears

A barricade to keep the demons at bay

A painted illusion

Meticulously arranged

Satiating the barrage of expectations hampered upon her

Void of meaning

Empty of happiness

It was always there

A smile

Never reaching her eyes

Never radiating from her soul...

Until you

It happened in an instant

Before my mind had time to fathom the alteration

My heart confessed

Craving your existence

It was not the frivolous evanescence of lust

For your face remained a mystery

But my soul...

My soul knew you

Ached for you

Loved you

Your essence bled into me

A quiddity of inimitable certitude

Through time and space

Through the hollow emptiness of heartbreak

A purity of becoming

Seeping into my core

Intricately weaving into the very fabric of my being

You stitched together the lacerated pieces of my hope

And made me whole

A bean

Tiny in such an infinite world

Rising above the demons of her past

Her soul burns bright

Brilliance of strength

Inexorable spirit

Fire flows through her veins

Benevolent beauty

Her heart holds the love of a thousand lifetimes

Given to those worthy

Unrestrained

We danced

Once upon a time

Under the tree where we shared our first kiss

Promises of love whispered against my ear

You held me

Our bodies so close

I could feel you across every inch of my skin

Every beat of your heart thrummed against my own

I fell into you

Whole

Alive

There were dreams

Blurred within the chaos

Still and quiet

Moments of silent reprieve known only to me

Moments for heart and soul to envisage

An escape

Emergent of a thousand lifetimes of anguish

Suffocating

Vindicating

Paid in full with blood and bone

You were there

Watching

Always on the periphery

Unwavering tranquility

A strength I never knew

A confession whispered into the æther

Waiting

For the dawn

Of my surrender

I watch

The waves crashing against the shore

My mind swimming

Floating within the salty depths of the ocean's tears

A gentle breeze

Kissing my cheeks

The scent of brine and seaweed

Permeating my senses

My hand

Enveloped in the warmth of your own

Keeping me rooted

Hearts entwined

My soul belongs to you

Always

With a tender caress

You cut me open

Peering inside

The imperfect edges of my quintessence

Rough and uneven

Weathered and damaged by time

Running your fingers over the grain

Counting the scars within my heart

Every line an open wound

Every knot a bleeding memory

You gather them close

One by one

Delicate treasures of intricate lace

The fibers of my soul

Belong only to you

Hurl me spiraling into darkness

Lose me beyond the wandering stars

Lay me twisted amongst the nettles

Sever clean my empty heart

Kiss away the tears

Glistening down my cheeks

Chase away the shadows

Ignite my soul to keep

Beneath hope's fractured moonbeams

Of dawn's unwavering break

Love me thru eternity

Between these lives I wait

I dream

During nights of silent serenity

Infrequent moments of temporary tranquility

A sweet surrender to safe and sound

Rising from the grave

Whispering my name

I sink beneath the darkness

Touch every aftershock of my heart's evisceration

Hesitant of the priority it never was

I find your face within the fragments

Hear your voice

A sojourner within my soul

Ethereal desire

Breathing in life

Beckoning me home

The flames are extinguished

Though my tears still coalesce with the ash

Sleepless nights

Searching through charred debris

Reaching through silence

Begging for your presence within the remnants of eternal anguish

I thirst for a way out

As emptiness settles between the broken contours of my soul

Fighting within myself

For a control perpetually absent from my grasp

Purging the marrow from inside my bones

I welcome any delusion of lucid thought

As my heart hemorrhages with an emotion I'm terrified to name

If I say it out loud

Will the words be acrid on my tongue?

Sour from a rejection I won't survive

My expectations are minimal

All I want

Is to give you my love

Earth shaking beneath my feet

A thunderbolt ablaze within my chest

Chaotic frenzy of seductive destruction

Flesh against flesh

Your lips leave a trail of fire scorched across my soul

Erratic heartbeat

Turbulent breath

A delicious whirlwind of syncopated rhythm

We plummet

My soul rests in his hands

My heart beats between his fingers

Every fiber of my life

My being

Lies at his mercy

I would give up everything

A thousand times over

For a single moment in his arms

A chance to cave to the desire

Simmering deep within

A chance to feel whole

To feel love

It started as a flutter

In the back of my mind

The tiniest little mote of a feeling

Spreading through bone and flesh

Taking root inside my heart

Burrowing into every nook

Every crevice

Until the only thing there

Was you

Bright and consuming

You devoured my love

She has never felt bonny

Unseen by this shapeless world

Plain

Simple

She hides away

Sharp angles

Pale skin

Smattered freckles

Yet...

Her mind is pure

Her soul

Loving

Her heart

Kind

Separated by a lifetime

Longing

Waiting

He sees her beauty

Tastes her tears

Loves

A lifetime exhausted

Hemorrhaging words of heartbreak across pages yellowed and aged

Faded by tears

Dried and salted beneath amorphous annihilation

Happiness taunting on the periphery

An abstraction of which I could not relate

Though I craved it so

Tasted it in tiny samples

Through diaphanous moments of ephemeral slumber

Memories of a life yet to prevail

But if words are magic

Transfusing from my soul

An effervescence flowing through my veins

Enchanting the iridescence radiating from your heart

They sit on my tongue

A honeydewed essence

Waiting for you to explore

You say I have bewitched you

But it is you

Dear Sir

Who have captivated my love

Has my heart been so wicked?

Every day unremitting

Clawing through the depths of my exile

Staring into the abyss of shattered dreams

Fractured beyond repair

Blinded by ideas torn apart

Lying shredded at my feet

Hope

A thought I dare not indulge

For fear of the staggering weight it holds

Imprisoned behind an ending purged of conception

Time fades to black

Kaleidoscope hallucinations invade my mind

Anesthetize

Paralyze

A moment for my soul to rest

Sweet reprieve beckoning me home

I close my eyes

And find you

He came to me in shadows

Whispering across my soul

A touch

A desire

An ache within the emptiness of my shattered remains

Igniting a fire within my veins

An ebb and flow of inclination and surrender

Delicious agony

Devouring my senses

Stealing the breath from my lungs

Obliterating the fragility of an insubstantial love

Drowning beneath a waterfall of longing

Beneath a deluge of new possibility

The peace shrouded within my heart

Desperate to break free

Numbness within my heart

Frozen beneath time and circumstance

Imprisoned behind an incessant perplexity of disconnect

Suffocating each breath

I drown under the weight of loneliness

Emptiness consuming since the inception of my existence

Abandoned perception of a beleaguered evanescence

My soul bleeds for you

Aches for you

Craves evocation

I awaken with your touch

Every variegation

A kaleidoscope of desire

Surging within my veins

Bursting with ethereal quintessence

I come alive

It was a picturesque obliteration of heart and mind

Chaos echoing through my head

Aftershocks reverberating through flesh and bone

The beats within my chest stutter beneath every wave

The sky above breathes ash

As day ignites into an obsidian nightmare

I shatter under the weight of my desolation

Pieces scattering amidst crystal tears of heartbreak

A staggering emptiness fills my veins

Vision blurring

Hope faltering

Until a voice from beyond the darkness

Gathering the remnants of my decimated soul

Offering solace

A place of shelter

Love

Cobalt gaze

Piercing souls

My heart knew yours before my eyes ever drank you in

Through infinite lifetimes of longing

As the blood coursing through my veins

I hold you

In every existence

Until the breath of time comes undone

Forever yours

The script of our love

Written in eternity

Soft melody of biphonic texture

Whispering harp within my soul

Aching tempo of glistening tears

Painting a ballad of flesh with gold

My heart thrums a heavy staccato

Your name a breath upon my lips

A Symphony of rhythm uniting

Piercing timbre of sultry lyrics

We crescendo

She dances beneath the euphoria of a resurrected heartbeat

Breathed to life by the dreams of time awakened

Pulsing through her veins

Every note reverberates with an ariose serenity

A melodious deluge of dulcet tranquility

Wrapped in the seraphic quintessence of his gaze

She sways to the rhythm of his voice

His words

Beckoning her forward

A canorous nexus of souls aligned

Within a Symphony of their restored forever

Ephemeral remembrance of saccharine delights

As smooth ambrosian opulence whispers across my tongue

A taste of efflorescence dripping from your lips

As redolent languor weaves a sweet Symphony within my soul

I feel you

A ripple within the fabric of time

A long-awaited imbrication of my heart's desire

Emollient to my desolation

With eloquence imbued hunger

A honeyed surrender of delicious agony

You claim me as your own

I amble through these memories

Filled with heartache and severed dreams

A landscape riddled with the tombstones of promises laid to rest

Beneath the chaos smashing inside my mind

I no longer feel the frenzied panic of a future out of reach

Of a present held in limbo

A voided ever after hangs upon the horizon

An obsolete never was disintegrates into ash behind me

There is only you

Filling my heart

A soft touch felt deep within the marrow of my bones

A voice

Whispering into my soul

Of love

I thirst for the relinquished tears

Bleeding from within your heart

As we drown beneath sonorous abandon

Sustained abreast a shared heartbreak

We demand nothing

Save for a mournful supplication of love

A mutual confession of souls

Suffocating underneath anguished torpidity

The blood in our veins

No longer stagnant

Surging

Igniting

Nourishing

A seed growing

Roots entwined

Adoration springs to life

A new forever

A tender devotion

We flourish

Heartache vanished within the emptiness of an obsidian sky

Lost amidst the shadows of an endless night

Forever searching

For an unknown frequency

A slit in the atmosphere

Leading me to you

I feel you within the iridescent glow of the flickering stars

Breathe in your light from the suffocating darkness

Words unspoken

Burning within my veins

Soul ablaze

With aureate awakening

The air ripples around me

A turquoise haze of breath held

A memory quivering within the atmosphere

Whisping through the delicate fingers of a subliminal heartbeat

I have been here before

Lost within this dream of ever waking sorrow

Floating within the effervescence of a haunted past

Alone I search

Scouring the emptiness

Teetering on the edge of purgation

For a feeling

A whisper from the shadows

To quiet my soul

Stumbling into a sphere of evanescent oblivion

Your voice brushes against my psyche

Alluring consciousness

Begging me home

We sit in quiet surrender

Breathe in the silence

My head on your shoulder

Fingers entwined

Words flutter through my mind

Delicate sweetness on the tip of my tongue

I savor the simplicity

Treasure these moments

A sugared calm seeping into my bones

A honeyed serenity absent until you

Sparkling luminescence dances amongst the branches

Glistening upon the canopy above

Twinkling whispers of radiance offer a welcoming embrace

I lean into you

The warmth of your presence enveloping me

So pure

So true

My darling love

My life

My home

She watches the world around her

A silent observer

Scars hidden behind iridescent beauty

Heartache masked beneath a gentle hope

Bones carved from steel

Blood imbued with unbreakable resolve

She knows all too well the evils hidden amidst the shadows

She's made friends with the demons who lurk within their darkness

Her eyes reveal the stories of a thousand lifetimes

Of eternity's unwavering survival

Of love's infinite splendor

Steal the fire from inside my veins

Bleed me dry

Drink the air from within my lungs

Leave me suffocating

Shatter my soul

Ravage my still beating heart

The broken shards of my life

Are at your mercy

A mosaic of sorrow

You savor each piece

Consume me wholly

Breathe into me

Back to life

I hover between this life and the next

Caught betwixt the end and a new beginning

A silhouette blurring into obscurity

A staccato heartbeat

Muffled by the chaotic rhythm of my tears

Light blossoms in the distance

A cerulean flame wrapping me in warmth

Amidst a fiery kiss

I alight

I hear your voice

Soft against my ear

Taste its melody

Sugary sweetness on the tip of my tongue

Your words

Fluttering across my mind

Every curve

Every angle

Every letter

A gentle caress

They flow through my veins

Ink staining my heart

Etching into my soul

A desire

So long dormant

A hope

So long laid to rest

Happiness

Finally

Within reach

Within the fibrous abdication of heart's abandon

She waits

Smoldering beneath the flames

Teetering along the fringe between heaven and hell

A forsaken entity

Neither angel nor demon

A quiddity of heart wrenching madness

Imprisoned by the tenebrous creatures of ravaged nightmares

She is relinquished of faith

Emptied of purpose

Renounced to her own devastation

But a glimmer of hope dances along the horizon

Incandescent longing beckoning across the distance

From a place beyond this devastating wasteland

A soul

Whispering her name

Guiding her home

There are secrets

Buried beneath the scars

Locked behind doors

Closed so long ago

The keys have tarnished and corroded past repair

Repair that would take a thousand lifetimes to shine

I sit within the chaos of my anguish

Trepidation coursing through my veins

Veins left open and bleeding by those who came before

Afraid to breathe

Afraid to move

As you explore every jagged edge of my heart's annihilation

Collocated by the universe

With unwavering patience

With unbounded devotion

Audacious to the demons plaguing my soul

You see me

Beyond the shattering heartbreak

Beyond the desolation

Feel the shuddering of my surrender

Surrender I willingly acquiesce

Without thought

Without hesitation

I am yours

Always

About the Author

Symphony Hale is a native California writer, chaser of dreams, wiper of messes, mom of 4.75. Writing is part of the very fabric of her DNA. For as long as she can remember, she's had stories and characters dancing around inside her head to an endless montage of love and laughter, heartbreak and suspense, and everything in between. Since 2017, she has been working as a ghost writer on novels ranging from Romance, to Cozy Mystery, to Paranormal, and many other genres. When she's not writing, she can be found chauffeuring kids around, doing WAY too many miles on her Peloton, and enjoying all of the beauty the world has to offer. She can be found at www.symphonyhale.com and on Twitter, Instagram, and Threads at @symphony_hale.

www.ingramcontent.com/pod-product-compliance
Lightning Source LLC
LaVergne TN
LVHW011910080426
835508LV00007BA/330